Murder

in the

Churchyard

This is by no means the first account of Rye's
most famous murder. The story is told in
different forms in every local history and in
various specially written booklets.
Much scholarly work has been done to
modify some of the more spectacular
elaborations. This version seeks to entertain
rather than inform.

Published 1997 by
Gungarden Books,
Rye, East Sussex, TN31 7HH

ISBN number 0 9517071 2 4

Printed by the Ditchling Press Ltd
Burgess Hill, Sussex

MURDER
in the
CHURCHYARD

The Story of Rye's most Infamous
Crime retold in pictures by

JOHN RYAN

Gungarden Books

It was a dark and stormy evening in March 1743.
The wind whistled through the buttresses of
Saint Mary's Church, and in the mean houses
huddled round Church Square the poorer people
of Rye stayed at home for fear of the weather.

But not everyone remained so
quiet. Alongside the quay, at
the foot of the steps beneath
the ancient Ypres Tower, lay
the ship of a young excise
officer, Lieutenant Lamb.

And he, for all that it was
such a wild night, was giving
a party on shipboard.

To it he had invited no less a person than his own father, James Lamb, the Mayor of Rye, whose family had become at that time one of the richest and best known in the town.

With a fortune based on a successful brewery,
they had built a fine house on the corner of
West Street. It had been here that, many years
earlier, James Lamb had entertained the King,
George the First …

who, stormbound when returning to England, had
been forced to land on the coast nearby. During the
King's stay, Lamb's wife had given birth to a son to
whom George, though he could barely speak a word
of English, had stood as Godfather.

But now James Lamb was a widower and that night he was in poor health. As he left his home to walk to his son's ship, he saw his brother-in-law Allen Grebell in the doorway of his house opposite.

'Allen,' he called, 'I'm a sick man this evening.
Why don't you go to the boy's dinner in my place?
You love parties, and I'm sure the lad will be just
as happy to see you as me.'

'Fair enough, James,' answered Grebell,
'but lend me your cloak. It's a foul night and I've no
desire to get soaked.' So Allen Grebell set off across
the churchyard wearing the Mayor's red cloak.

It was a good party. Lieutenant Lamb was delighted
to welcome his fun-loving uncle on board in place of
his father.

It was well past midnight when Allen Grebell, happily wined and dined, set off on his short journey home.

Then, as always in Rye, gossip travelled fast, and for one of the townsfolk the affairs of the Lamb family that night were to be of special interest.

John Breeds, a butcher and innkeeper, nursed a deep and unforgiving grudge against the Mayor, who had once, as Magistrate, fined him for giving short measure.

That night, Breeds, after a heavy bout of drinking, vowed revenge.

His enemy would, he
knew, be bound to
return from the party
through the churchyard,
only a few steps from
his own home in the
Flushing Inn.

So to the churchyard
Breeds made his unsteady
way, to lie in wait.

For an hour or more he sat, concealed by a buttress, drinking steadily.

Then came the sound of the footsteps he was expecting.

Dimly he saw the approaching figure, half lit by a lantern held in a rather shaky hand. Breeds was fuddled with alcohol but he recognised the Mayor's red cloak.

His chance had come.
With a yell of fury he
dashed out, brandishing
his butcher's knife …

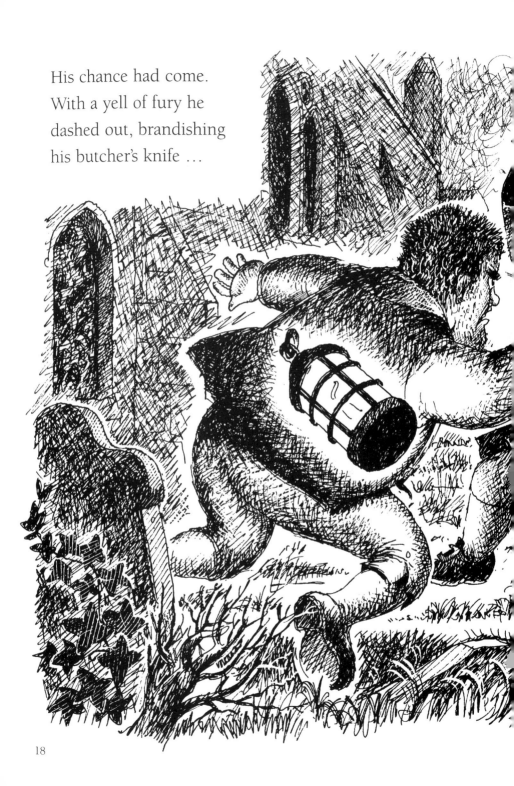

… and drove it fiercely
into the chest of – not
James Lamb of course, but
Allen Grebell.

But his victim had drunk too much himself to
realise what had happened. Some other fuddled
fellow had, he thought, collided with him in the
churchyard. He stumbled back the short distance
to his house, sent the servant who had waited up
for him to bed ...

... and settled himself
in front of the fire.

Still unaware of the deep
wound in his chest, he
fell asleep.

Meanwhile, in the house
opposite, James Lamb was having a bad night.
Three times he dreamt that his dead wife
came to him and cried …

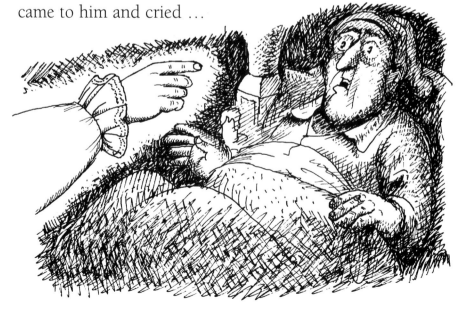

'Something terrible has happened to Allen! Go to his aid, for God's sake.'

Twice Lamb disregarded the dream. The third time he rose, hurried over the road …

… and found he was too late. His brother-in-law had bled to death.

At first it was thought, when the alarm was raised, that the servant had killed his master, but then it became known …

… that Breeds the butcher, barely clothed and by now half-crazed with drink, had spent the rest of the night dancing round the town shouting, 'BUTCHERS *should* kill LAMBS!'

Then his blood-stained
knife was found in the
churchyard, with his name
carved on the handle. Probably
it was only when he was arrested that he
realised he had killed the wrong man.

It was strange, perhaps, that the judge at Breeds' trial
was the very man that the accused had tried to kill.
But the evidence against the butcher was overwhelming.

He pleaded insanity, maybe with good reason, but to no
avail. It was said that when sentenced to be hanged he
turned to Lamb and shouted. 'It was not for Mr Grebell I
meant it. It was for you and I'd murder you now if I could!'

John Breeds' last days were spent chained in a cell in the gloomy Ypres prison tower.

In June, more than two months after the murder, he took his last drink at the Flushing Inn, which had once been his.

Then they hanged him outside the Strand Gate
before a great crowd of spectators.

For twenty years or more the rotting body was exposed on the Marsh in a specially made iron frame, as a dreadful warning to passers-by.

This was the custom of the time. Later the bones were transferred to a corner of Saint Mary's Church.

There, it is said, they were ransacked by the old women of the town, ground to powder, and sold as a cure for rheumatism and Heaven knows what else.

At last, only part of the skull remained. It hangs to this day in its iron cage in an attic in the Town Hall, a sinister reminder of Rye's most notorious murder.

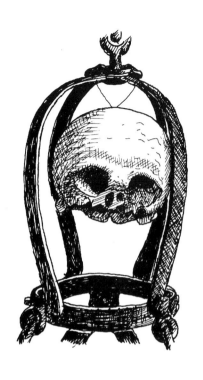

*So is told the story of Lamb, Grebell and Breeds.
As with so many tales, it has been lovingly
embellished with the passage of time, and details
have been added which may be untrue. Certainly,
however, the murder took place. Allen Grebell's
tomb with its inscription, 'Killed by a sanguinary
butcher', is in the north aisle of the Church, and
the grim relic in the Town Hall is proof of the
basic truth of the story.*